FAITH
THAT CONQUERS:
The Key to Kingdom Blessings

NICHOLAS KISAKYE

KHAMEL
PUBLISHING

This book has been published in print, e-format and sold on Amazon.com by KHAMEL Publishing.

Visit us on the web at:
www.khamelpublishing.com

ISBN: 978-9970-9453-1-3
2nd Edition, December 2015

© Nicholas Kisakye 2015

All rights reserved. No part of this book may be reproduced in any form or by any means without the prior consent of the Publisher, excepting brief quotes used in reviews.

Author's Contact:

Nicholas Kisakye
P. O. Box 8484, Kampala, Uganda
Email: nicholas@returntozion.org
Tel: +256 706334862 or +256 772338586
Website: www.returntozion.org

Scriptural references in this book were made from the 1986 New International Version (NIV).

Table of Contents

DEDICATION	II
FOREWORD	III
SCRIPTURAL REFLECTION	V
ACKNOWLEDGEMENTS	VI
INTRODUCTION	1
GOD'S DESIRE TO BUILD A MIGHTY KINGDOM	3
THE REVELATION OF THE KINGDOM	15
THE POWER OF FAITH	21
THE IMPORTANCE OF A SOLID FOUNDATION	29
ENTERING HIS REST	39
ALL POSSIBLE WITH GOD	45
PROMISES ARE LIKE SEEDS	53
ARE WE READY TO POSSESS THE LAND?	61

DEDICATION

This book is dedicated to every child of God who, for one reason or another, is experiencing challenges that seem impossible to overcome. May the faith you develop, as a result of reading this book, give you the long-awaited victory, in Jesus' name.

FOREWORD

ONE GREAT REVIVALIST, Mzee Eliezer Mugimba, once told me that faith laughs at impossibility. There are situations in our lives that look like mountains before us. But faith laughs at them! Without faith, as Christians, we struggle so much in the flesh to no avail. But once faith has stepped in, these mountains begin to crumble. We begin to view them as mere anthills that we can climb. Indeed, the grace of God empowers us to climb them.

Faith has a great role to play in our Christian walk with the Lord. It keeps us on the right pathway to our God-ordained destiny. Faith enables us to put all our trust in the Lord. That way, He gives us the hope to trust that He is in control of every situation we encounter, even those that threaten our very existence. With faith we cannot accept to be discouraged by anything. Faith makes our eyes stay focused on the God of heaven who promised to be with us till the end of time.

The power of faith enables us to gain what God has prepared for us both in the Heavenly Kingdom and in the earthly Kingdom. This is why, in Luke 17:5-6, the apostles of Jesus asked Him to increase their faith. But Jesus replied, *"If you have faith as small as a mustard seed, you can say to this mulberry tree, 'Be uprooted and planted in the sea,' and it will obey you!"* Can you imagine commanding a tree and it is uprooted from one place and planted in another? That's the conquering faith that this book is talking about.

In this book, Nicholas provides compelling evidence for people of God to know that having Jesus Christ in their own lives as Lord and Saviour, and having faith in Him, opens doors to heavenly blessings that one cannot count and finish. This is in line with what St Paul says in Philippians 4:19: *"And my God will supply all your needs according to his glorious riches in Christ Jesus."* Therefore, without faith, we labour in vain.

Nicholas also brings out clearly the fact that there are those who have known Jesus and continue to seek Him, but are not aware of the principles of receiving from God's Kingdom in order to inherit its blessings. He labours to help the reader discover ways in which he/she can fully tap what is in the heavenly realm and make it real in his/her physical realm through faith.

The book emphasises the ways in which our faith can be built, focusing so much on the Word of God. St Paul says in Romans 10:17-18, *"Consequently, faith comes from hearing the message, and the message is heard through the word of Christ."* This is very true. There is a special place for God's Word in building our faith in Him, and experiencing His Kingdom in our work and worship.

Reading this book is worth your time, effort and money. Nicholas' candid style of presentation of the principles in this book will not only make the reader more relevant to God's Kingdom purposes, but also steer him/her on the highway to fulfilling God's mission in his/her life for the glory of God. This will of course require the reader to practice the principles in order to enjoy the riches of His glory in Christ Jesus.

I therefore highly recommend this book to all who seek to grow, enjoy fullness of life and also serve the Lord Jesus more effectively and relevantly in their lifetime.

RT REV. NATHAN AHIMBISIBWE
Bishop, South Ankole Diocese.
Ntungamo, Uganda.

~ SCRIPTURAL REFLECTION ~

"...we are not those who shrink back and
are destroyed, but those who
believe and are saved."

(HEBREWS 10:39)

ACKNOWLEDGEMENTS

I WILL BEGIN by expressing my heartfelt gratitude to the Lord who called me into ministry and has been faithful in providing for me both spiritually and physically. Accomplishing this book project has been by His grace and providence.

Special thanks go out to Rt Rev. Nathan Ahimbisibwe, Bishop of South Ankole Diocese, who believed in this book and has authoritatively recommended it for the readers by writing its Foreword. May God give you long life.

I am very grateful to my wife, Margaret, and to our children Justine, Eve, Andrew, Monica, Elizabeth, Priscilla and Jean, who stood with me during tough times through which God revealed some of the insights that I share in this book. Monica also gave me all the support I needed in the process of developing the manuscript. My daughter, Monica, and my wife, Margaret, specifically, helped in the process of putting the ideas together.

I appreciate Andrew Tapie Musinguzi's efforts in encouraging me to write my thoughts and experiences. I also thank Robert Bake of World of Inspiration and Melissa Kyeyune of KHAMEL Publishing for publishing the different editions of this book.

Sincere thanks to Humphrey Puule and his wife Aisha for the great support and encouragement. I appreciate the support from Kampala Revival Fellowship, especially Gen. Elly Tumwiine and John Musinguzi. And to all my friends who in one way or the other contributed towards making this project a success, may God fill you with every good and perfect gift.

Lastly, allow me thank you dear reader for without you reading this book, my efforts would not yield the desired fruits. May God richly bless you as you read on.

INTRODUCTION

THE CREATION STORY presented in Genesis chapter 1 reveals that God was pleased with whatever He created. After creating the universe and everything in it, He saw that it was all good. Some versions say He was pleased by whatever He saw. Thus, by default, everything around us is supposed to be good. We were meant to have good families, good businesses, good jobs, good relationships, good leadership, good neighbourhoods, a good environment, e.t.c. That's how God's Kingdom was originally designed.

However, when Adam and Eve sinned, humanity fell short of God's glory and began to hide away from His Kingdom. That is how we lost our dominion over all creation. And so we started to lose the benefits of the children of the Kingdom. We started to live like orphans. We lost our position of being princes and princesses in our Father's Kingdom. That's how we began to live in lack, fear, bondage and despair.

But because God could not accept to lose the humanity that He had created in His own image, He had to figure out a mechanism of saving us. Throughout the Old Testament we see Him implementing several strategies to reconcile man back to Himself. He made covenants such as that with Noah, that with Abraham and that with the Israelites through Moses. But that was not enough. He spoke through prophets with a message calling humanity to get converted to Him. That too was not enough. Eventually, in the fullness of time, He sent His own Son to die on the cross and pull humanity back into the Kingdom. The Gospel of John 1:12 makes it clear that all those who believed in Jesus, He gave them the power to become children of God, which makes us princes and princesses in our Father's Kingdom. It is important to remember that this right to become children of God is not based on ethnicity or human effort but only God's supernatural work driven by His immeasurable love. To those who believe in Him, He adopts as His own children who from then on enjoy all the abundant and inexhaustible privileges of royalty.

Unfortunately, some people today have not yet allowed Jesus to bring them back into God's Kingdom, yet that is why He lowered Himself to come into the world and become like one of us. It's my heart's desire and most fervent prayer that they will find Him. But there are also those who have known Jesus and continue to seek Him, but are not aware of the principles of receiving from God's Kingdom in order to inherit its blessings. That's the reason I wrote this book – to help us discover the ways in which we can fully tap what's in the heavenly realm and make it ours in the physical realm.

It's my hope that as you read this book and interact with the scriptures and the various experiences that are shared, you will have a new mindset that will work as a master key to open doors of blessings in your life, your family, your workplace and your entire world. Let this book be your companion, a devotional of sorts, so that you can get God's daily guidance that will enable you keep your life, work, career, business, relationships and ambitions tuned to the Will and Principles of God so that no matter what you go through you will keep winning in this world. It is indeed good news to know that this winning that is rooted in Jesus Christ does not stop here. It extends into eternity, beginning with the banquet with our Father and King in Heaven; a feasting in glory that is from everlasting to everlasting!

~ CHAPTER 1 ~

GOD'S DESIRE TO BUILD A MIGHTY KINGDOM

GOD IS ESTABLISHING a Kingdom much larger than anything man has ever seen. The strength and power of this Kingdom has its root in the spiritual realm but it extends its manifestation into the visible physical sphere of man.[1]

God's authority spans through it and operates across both heaven and earth. Everything that comes to be on earth has its origin in heaven. Over and over in the scriptures, we see this: that God is Spirit. He declares His Will in the Spirit. Once spoken, God's Will is established in the spiritual realm. It then slowly takes shape in the physical realm on earth, in His time.

---

[1] Matthew 16:18: "And I tell you that you are Peter, and on this rock I will build my church, and the gates of Hades will not overcome it."

At the apex of this Kingdom sits Jesus Christ. He and He alone has total authority over the Kingdom of God.

Scripture declares: *"He made known to us the mystery of His Will according to His good pleasure, which He purposed in Christ, to be put in effect when the times Will have reached their fulfilment – to bring all things in Heaven and on earth together under one head, even Christ"* (Ephesians 1: 9-10).

We also read in Ephesians 1:22-23 that *"God placed all things under His feet and appointed Him to be head over everything for the church, which is His body, the fullness of Him who fills everything in every way."*

The nature of God's Kingdom is eternal. Unlike the empires of men which rise and fall with time, God's Will lasts forever. The Psalmist declares, *"Your rule is eternal and you are king forever"* (Psalm 145:13). God also declares: *"Of the increase of His government and peace, there shall be no end"* (Isaiah 9:7). Indeed as we read in Romans 11:29, God's gift and His call are irrevocable. It is thus clear that everything that flows from this Kingdom is everlasting. Hence, those who are part of this Kingdom receive eternal life, and enjoy eternal blessings.

~ A Kingdom that Lacks Nothing ~

FOR A MOMENT imagine a hole that is so deep that you cannot see the bottom. Then imagine such a hole full of assorted treasures, with billions of cash and all other supplies. Such is the nature of God's Kingdom.

The various kingdoms that have existed have at one point or another, experienced unmet needs and even acute shortages. God's Kingdom on the other hand is incapable of lack. Once we are in this Kingdom we have everything that we need to live a happy, purposeful and meaningful life. There is a scripture that confirms: *"His divine power has given us everything we need for life and godliness…"* (2 Peter 1:3).

In another scripture, St Paul declares: *"Praise be to the God and Father of our Lord Jesus Christ, who has blessed us in the heavenly realms with every spiritual blessing in Christ"* (Ephesians 1:3). It was no mistake that while writing this scripture, Paul the Apostle used the word "every". He was trying to show us that nothing we needed was outside of God's provision and power. Just like St Peter used the word 'everything' in the scripture above – all to mean the same thing.

All that God intends for us begins in His Will. Once spoken, His Will is established in the heavenly realm in form of spiritual blessings. He lets us know the Will He has for our earthly life through Prayer, and meditation on His Word. This way, we know how to pray, in accordance to His Will, so that His Will is what we speak back to Him in our prayers and petitions. This is the process by which God's spoken Will for us, that has been established in the heavens becomes manifested in our physical reality.

~ God's words are never idle ~

THE WORLD WE see was created by God's word. He would simply say "Let there be…" and it would come into existence. Once God has spoken, His words must achieve the purpose for which they were sent. Isaiah 55:10-11 says: *"As the rain and the snow come down from heaven, and do not return to it without watering the earth and making it bud and flourish, so that it yields seed for the sower and bread for the eater, so is my word that goes out from my mouth: It will not return to me empty, but will accomplish what I desire and achieve the purpose for which I sent it."*

In Revelation 21:5-6 this is what we read: *"He who was seated on the throne said, 'I am making everything new!' Then He said, 'Write this down, for these words are trustworthy and true'. He said to me: 'It is done. I am the Alpha and the Omega, the Beginning and the End. To him who is thirsty I will give to drink without cost from the spring of the water of life."*

God, through Moses, spoke to the Israelites thus: *"Take to heart all the words I have solemnly declared to you this day, so that you may command your children to obey carefully all the words of this law. They are not just idle words for you- they are your life. By them you will live long in the land you are crossing the Jordan to possess"* (Deuteronomy 32:46-47).

Once God activates something by speaking His Will, it is a done deal. Our responsibility, as children of God, is to find out what that Will is and how we can be part of the process of making it our physical reality. His Will has been written; our duty is to find it, read it, know what has been given to us and then go possess it. A good example of this in the Word is Joseph. You'll find his story in Genesis, Chapters 37 to 50. When Joseph received the dreams about his future, God's plans for his life were already sealed in the spiritual realm and were in motion. Joseph only needed to believe God and trust that regardless of time and events, God would surely bring it to pass.

When we claim what is rightfully ours or seek God for an answer we do so not as beggars or thieves. We are only asking for that which has been legally awarded to us as sons and heirs.

Caleb knew who he was in God's Will. He knew what his stake was as an Israelite and he boldly took claim of it. According to Joshua 14:6-15, he said: *"You know what the Lord said to Moses the man of God at Kadesh Barnea about you and me. I was forty years old when Moses the servant of the Lord sent me from Kadesh Barnea to explore the land. And I brought him back a report according to my convictions, but my brothers who went up with me made the hearts of the people melt with fear. I, however, followed the Lord my God wholeheartedly. So, on that day Moses swore to me, 'The land on which your feet have walked will be your inheritance and that of your children forever, because you have followed the Lord my God wholeheartedly.' Now then, just as the Lord promised, He has kept me alive for forty-five years since the time He said this to Moses, while Israel moved about in the desert. So here I am today, eighty-five years old! I am still as strong today as the day Moses sent me out; I'm just as vigorous to go out to battle now as I was then. Now give me this hill country that the Lord promised me that day. You yourself heard then that the Anakites were there and their cities were large and fortified, but, the Lord helping me, I will drive them out just as He said."*

Indeed the claim had to be honoured. *"Then Joshua blessed Caleb son of Jephunneh and gave him Hebron as his inheritance."*

Despite the years spent in the wilderness and through all the hardships of the desert crossing, Caleb never forgot God's promise to him. He was so convinced of his success that he contended with occupied territories that others had shunned knowing that because God had made a promise to him, nothing would stand in the way of him receiving what was his.

When God makes a promise or releases our provision, all we need to do, as children, is receive it or at least find out what part we can play in the process of doing so. God has written it down in His word. It is a culmination of all His good intent and is binding on Him. It is our responsibility to search this word, know what belongs to us and then go out and boldly take a hold of it.

~ Participating in God's Plan ~

GOD WANTS TO work with us in His Kingdom. He wants us to play an active role in His divine nature. *"His divine power has given us everything we need for life and godliness through our knowledge of him who called us by his own glory and goodness. Through these he has given us his very great and precious promises, so that through them you may participate in the divine nature and escape the corruption in the world caused by evil desires"* (2 Peter 1:3-4).

The first step in this process is to believe in the Gospel and to accept the free gift of salvation. This is what many know as being Born Again or saved. We are Born Again, that is, made new by the Spirit of God, when we accept Jesus as Lord.

The opportunity for new birth is open to everybody. When we embrace Jesus as saviour, the Holy Spirit lives within us and begins to transform our nature into that of our father God. *"Flesh gives birth to flesh, but the Spirit gives birth to spirit"* (John 3:6).

When we are Born Again we are reconciled to the divine just as we were meant to be before the fall of Adam. Once we are born of God, we take on His magnificent characteristics, including but not limited to the fact that we begin to walk by faith and not by sight. We learn to speak life into dead things, and in His power, we begin to see things that are not yet a reality as if they are. To achieve this, we speak, not our own words, but His words, His great and precious promises back to Him with conviction. This is called faith. *"Now faith is being sure of what we hope for and certain of what we do not see"* (Hebrews 11:1).

"As it is written: 'I have made you a father of many nations.' He is our father in the sight of God, in whom he believed—the God

Faith that Conquers 9

who gives life to the dead and calls things that are not as though they were" (Roman 4:17). This is a clear description, one of the many manifestations of God's divine nature.

We are Born Again, by the Word of God, by God's Spirit, and by faith. To understand this process let's learn from Jesus' own birth. The story as outlined in Luke 1:26-38: *"In the sixth month, God sent the angel Gabriel to Nazareth, a town in Galilee, to a virgin pledged to be married to a man named Joseph, a descendant of David. The virgin's name was Mary. The angel went to her and said, 'Greetings, you who are highly favoured! The Lord is with you.' Mary was greatly troubled at his words and wondered what kind of greeting this might be. But the angel said to her, 'Do not be afraid, Mary, you have found favour with God. You will be with a child and give birth to a son, and you are to give him the name Jesus. He will be great and will be called the Son of the Most High. The Lord God will give him the throne of his father David, and he will reign over the house of Jacob forever; his Kingdom will never end.' 'How will this be,' Mary asked the angel, 'since I am a virgin?' The angel answered, 'The Holy Spirit will come upon you, and the power of the Most High will overshadow you. So the holy one to be born will be called the Son of God. Even Elizabeth your relative is going to have a child in her old age, and she who was said to be barren is in her sixth month. For nothing is impossible with God.' 'I am the Lord's servant,' Mary answered. 'May it be to me as you have said.' Then the angel left her."*

There's something we need to understand clearly: Mary being of traditional Jewish upbringing was very concerned. How could the angel's words come true? She had never been with a man. How would God's promise to her be fulfilled? This had never happened before in history. But the angel assured her how the Holy Spirit would come upon her and the power of the Most High would overshadow her. Being filled with the kind of faith that conquers,

Mary accepted and submitted to the Promise and Will of God even when she couldn't fully understand it. Not long after Mary was pregnant!

I would like to pause here and point out how pivotal the Word is to many of the things God desires to do. From the creation of man and the world in Genesis to the Second Coming of Jesus in Revelation, words play a crucial role in the unfolding of God's Kingdom. Everything starts from God's word including being Born Again.

To be Born Again we must first hear the Gospel. We then accept it, believe it and confess it with our own words. *"...if you confess with your mouth, "Jesus is Lord," and believe in your heart that God raised him from the dead, you will be saved. For it is with your heart that you believe and are justified, and it is with your mouth that you confess and are saved."* This we read in Romans 10:9.

It is then that the Holy Spirit comes to dwell in and with us. We have received a new birth and scripture declares us a new creation. *"Therefore, if anyone is in Christ, he is a new creation; the old has gone, the new has come"* (2 Corinthians 5:17). This new birth brings us into a new family, with Jesus as our elder brother. *"Both the one who makes men holy and those who are made holy are of the same family. So Jesus is not ashamed to call them brothers"* (Hebrews 2:11). We become co-heirs with Him (Christ) in the Kingdom and are therefore entitled to all the wealth of our Father, the King. *"Now if we are children, then we are heirs—heirs of God and co-heirs with Christ..."* (Romans 8: 17).

But how can we inherit blessings we are not convinced exist? We must believe with all our heart that they are real. Once we do that, we can experience the joy and peace that are rooted in the knowledge that we have access to blessings beyond compare. This is faith. This same faith is what moves us to speak life into every situation. Through our utterances we give life to every situation we face. This power of life and death is manifested in the words we choose to speak over our lives and situations. *"From the fruit of his mouth a man's stomach is filled; with the harvest from his lips he is satisfied. The tongue has the power of life and death, and those who love it will eat its fruit"* (Proverbs 18:20-21). We should guard our speech and endeavour to confess only that which is good.

~ My Experience of God's Supernatural Providence ~

MY LIFE IS evidence of the fact that God's Kingdom lacks nothing. I am confident of this because I have seen God provide for my family and I in ways that defy human understanding.

Before I accepted Christ, I ran several successful businesses. I sold timber from Mahogany, one of Africa's hard wood trees. My businesses were doing well and turning in a healthy profit. Who could have guessed that a year later I would not even be able to buy food let alone the salt with which to season it.

A year after my conversion, the stores in which I kept my timber in three different towns were robbed. In that same year a garden of passion fruits burned to the ground, just as I had started to market the soon to be harvested produce. And like Job, calamity was to visit me a third time. I later found out that the farm I had purchased had been sold to another party as well.

A long legal battle for the land ensued, which I eventually lost. This would not be the last time that disaster visited me. The car which was being used to coordinate my businesses perished in an accident. Then I lost a tractor to one of my partners.

The turmoil of that year left me crushed and destitute. I could not even afford bus fare to town. I was forced to walk a distance of 5kms whenever I needed to go to town. Many times I used side streets in an attempt to avoid meeting any of my former acquaintances. I was ashamed to be seen in such a pitiable situation.

Unable to provide for my family, I turned to my wife. She shouldered the burden of providing for the family. This was one of the toughest choices I have had to make. Every man takes pride in being able to take care of his wife and children. The house we lived in was part of her entitlement as a teacher. In those days, the government provided free housing for teachers. However, even this small joy was to be short lived. The government soon changed policy and all teachers were required to pay rent. This felt like Satan's masterstroke. How would we be able to pay rent, pay school fees and feed ourselves on what was already a meagre teacher's salary?

At the time, with my sudden free time I had started volunteering with the Province of the Church of Uganda in the Missions' Department. It was my only solace. But as things worsened, my wife asked that I look for a job in place of volunteering.

Watching my family begin to starve, indeed finding a job seemed like the most logical answer. I spoke with the Province and informed them that I would not be able to volunteer with them anymore. Knowing my circumstances they blessed and released me.

No sooner had I made that decision than a great weight settled upon me. I felt the entire world resting upon my shoulders. Now, uncertain of my choice, I went to God in prayer. I fasted and sought clarity from God. On the last day of my appointed fast, I received a dream which I was unable to interpret, perhaps due to my spiritual immaturity at the time. I was undeterred and began to pray, this time for wisdom and interpretation of the dream.

The next day, as I waited to pick my children from school, I heard a voice direct me to Isaiah 58:11. I got out my pocket Bible and looked it up. It promises: *"The Lord will guide you always; He will satisfy your needs in a sun-scorched land and will strengthen your frame. You will be like a well-watered garden, like a spring whose waters never fail."*

I was elated. I paced back and forth in the compound oblivious to those around me. I was just so happy that finally I had a word from the Lord for my situation. I was still destitute but that did not matter. God had spoken. In the spiritual realm, things had changed. Later that day I shared what had happened with my wife and told her I would not abandon the Mission field. From then on, I made a point to continually remind myself of what the Lord had promised. In prayer, I spoke it back to the Lord always.

That promise was the start of God's provision! All we needed was provided for from clothing to food. In the years that followed, we were even able to buy the flat that we once struggled to pay rent for. Later, we were also able to move to another home with more room for our growing family.

I look back at my days of fear and I am ashamed because now I see Gods faithfulness. Why did I ever doubt Him? We know now that the Kingdom of God is a reality and is able to meet every need of everyone's need. God's Kingdom lacks nothing!

~ God's Strange Ways ~

IT IS VITAL to note that, sometimes, when God wants to teach us to live by the supernatural, from heaven, He can allow the natural things to first fail. For instance, when God wanted to teach the children of Israel how to live by the Word from His mouth, before they could receive manna from heaven, He first took them into the desert (Deuteronomy 8:1-3). In this context, manna represents the physical things we can see and touch. God wants us to learn that He can supernaturally provide every need when we learn to unlock our heavenly blessings through his Word.

In Numbers 11:4-32, the children of Israel wanted meat. But, instead of turning to Him and asking, they just complained. Moses himself also started complaining even when God promised that He would supply them with meat: God answered him: *"Is the Lord's arm too short? You will now see whether or not what I say will come true."* Numbers 11:31 reports God sending a wind that drove quail from the sea. The quail was all around the camp up to about 3ft above the ground. It was so plentiful and so easily accessible that even children, the sick and the lame could catch and eat. He supplied meat to a population of close to a million people for a whole month! God indeed provided exceedingly, abundantly, far beyond Moses' expectation.

We see the same situation with Jesus' disciples in Luke 5:17. These men were professional fishermen, with all the skills to catch fish, but for a whole night they did their best and caught nothing. All their skills and ideas had failed, until Jesus showed up and gave them a Word. At His Word, which they believed, they cast their nets into the deep, as instructed, and the number of fish they caught was so amazing that the nets were about to get torn. They needed extra help to handle the catch! Imagine that!

~ CHAPTER 2 ~

THE REVELATION OF THE KINGDOM

IN THE OLD Testament, the favour of God was limited to God's chosen people – the Israelites – through the Abrahamic Covenant. However, today all who accept it are welcome because of the New Covenant under Jesus Christ. All who believe in Jesus are welcomed into the family of God and are therefore privy to the blessings accorded to the lineage of Abraham, Isaac and Jacob.

The fruits of God's Kingdom and the principles that govern it are not secret. There is no greater evidence of this than the fact that the crucifixion, the resurrection and ascension were public events witnessed by many. It was not something that was done in secret before one man like God did with Abraham or with many of the Old Testament figures. In fact the followers of Jesus were commanded <u>to go and share</u> this "good news" with all men in the entire world.[2]

---

[2] Matthew 28:19: "Therefore go and make disciples of all nations, baptizing them in

So the Kingdom is open to all and is governed by principles. If you desire to thrive and live in peace with a particular people or community, you must endeavour to learn the norms of that society and to live by them.

When we understand these principles and apply them, God surely manifests Himself in our daily lives. We begin to see our effort bearing fruit and favour before God and before men.

~ Not a Secret Anymore ~

WHEN MEN IMAGINE God, He is imagined as this aloof bearded man scowling down at us waiting to rain punishment on us for the slightest infraction. He is painted as a master who asks for the impossible knowing we cannot achieve it just so He can punish us. It is this prevailing view that leaves many of us afraid and distant from God.

This has never been further from the truth. God is not interested in hiding anything from us. He does not desire that we stumble around blindly. If anything He does all in His power to see that we have all that we need to live a fulfilled and content life.

Throughout the Bible, God sent His prophets and His many servants to reveal His Will to His people that they would follow Him. It was the reason behind the writing of the scriptures and the reason He sent His Son to die for all mankind. Throughout this book, you will notice how much emphasis is put on the Word of God because I believe knowing God's Word is knowing God. The more we know, the more we understand God. Through His Word, we see clearer the purpose of our life just like peering through binoculars allows us to see further ahead in our path.

The blueprint for our destiny is built into God's Word. As

we seek Him through the study of His Word, He reveals more to us. Through the revelation of the Holy Spirit, God is able to continually reveal more of Himself to His own. It is this blueprint that we can use as a guide to experience the manifestation of what God has already secured for us in the spiritual realm. Scripture is full of innumerable promises applicable to every aspect of life. They are the key that allow us to be part of the divine nature, which is God's very essence.

Life is busy and full of distractions. It is easy to lose sight of these truths as we go through our daily routines. We have to discipline ourselves to be tuned to God's frequency in order, not just to recognize, but to be able to apply the guidelines of God's supernatural blueprint. It is this discipline that gives us insight into the things of the Spirit and God's plan, thus giving us the courage to stand firm in our claim to the Promised Land, until the day we take hold of it.

My son is a pastor in the United Kingdom. In the course of his ministry, a young student, a beautiful lady from the United Arab Emirates received Christ. Like all converts from Islam, her family was not thrilled by this news. She turned to the church for refuge.

In the course of sharing the Christian walk, my son fell in love with her. He soon proposed to her. This news, understandably, was not well received by her family. Not only had she denounced her Islamic upbringing, but she dared to marry a non-Muslim. This was an affront to her family. To them it was the ultimate betrayal.

The two knew they wanted to live for God together in marriage, but they had two families to deal with, that did not trust their choice. I had misgivings about my son, who is in full time ministry, marrying a girl who was originally a Muslim. What if she backslid and frustrated his Ministry. Would she raise their children in the fear and knowledge of God? What did she know about being a wife to a pastor? How could she be a suitable helper to my son?

My son and his soon-to-become bride endured our misgivings, holding onto their faith in God and onto their love for each other. They anticipated the worst. You can therefore imagine our skepticism when we were invited to the UAE to discuss their marriage and receive approval from her family.

Like all parents, we were doubtful. We had read and heard of many terrible things done to women and the families of those that dared convert from Islam. We wondered if this invitation could be the hand of God. Perhaps He had given them a change of heart? Many a friend and colleague advised us against travelling and who could blame them? We too had our doubts and fears. It was tough.

I sought out my son. We discussed the possible outcomes if he went through with his plan to visit. He insisted on going and would not be dissuaded. He loved his fiancé and believed she was the wife God had given him. He hoped that as his father, I would stand with him, as a reflection of my love for him. I was torn in two. A father's responsibility is both to keep his children safe and at the same time be their number one encourager. I did not know which of the two God required me to be.

Troubled, I wondered why of all the women my son had chosen her? What had influenced his choice? Would she make a good wife for my son? I believe that miles away, my son's father-in-law was grappling with the same thoughts.

Confused and lost, I sought God in prayer as was my practice. I took to God all my questions, doubts and fears. I needed clear leading; Were we or were we not to go to the Emirates? As I prayed and fasted I had a dream. Through this dream and its scriptural interpretation, I received my answer from God. He set all my fears to rest. In doing so, I knew that this girl would be good for my son. God was not against it, why should I be? What did I know? God also assured me that He would grant me favour before our hosts. The dream revealed that there would be tensions, but that God would miraculously lead us to a mutual peaceful and respectful conclusion to the matter. So, despite the warnings from close friends, my wife and I agreed that I would travel. My son and I went about making the necessary preparations. This was no longer simply about a marriage but also a test of my trust in my God.

This resolve was quickly tested. As we sat in the living room of my soon-to-be daughter-in-laws' parents, tempers flared and voices were raised. They said the only way my son could marry their daughter was if he converted to Islam and she renounced Christianity. I could understand this, but I held tightly to the hope that the word God had spoken to me would come to pass.

In all this chaos there was one glimmer of hope. My son's fiancée stood firm. She did not let the heightened emotions move her as she openly declared her commitment to Jesus. I sat there with sympathy for my colleague on the opposite side of the room. I understood her family's anger and disappointment.

It was so tense that you could almost cut the tension with a knife. But through it all God was faithful to His Word and promise.

My son did get married to the woman of his dreams and her parents even flew to London to attend the wedding and invited us back to the Emirates to be received officially into the family. My son and his wife are happily married, with two wonderful children.

What a miracle!

~ Never Underestimate God's Revelation ~

THE OUTCOME OF my son's story is clear evidence that God kept His Word. At the end of the day I was rejoicing just as He said I would be. I trusted Him even in the face of personal peril and with absolutely no idea of how God was planning to work this out in my favour. My duty was to believe that He would do what He said He would do. *"And we know that in all things God works for the good of those who love him, who have been called according to his purpose"* (Romans 8:28).

It does not matter what you face in life. Commit to seeking the face of the Lord for a word and when you do hear this word, hang on for dear life with all that you have. Do not give up. Do not despair. Do not lose hope. It will come to pass. Jesus tells us that even faith as small as a mustard seed will move mountains. So whatever measure of faith you think you have, use it as your anchor to the promise God has given you.

It's an undeniable truth that God does guide us along our path in life. To some, He shall give an almost complete plan while others it's bits and pieces. He is always speaking to us. *"If the Lord delights in a man's way, he makes his steps firm"* (Psalm 37:23). This assurance should strengthen our resolve not to walk in our own knowledge. Allow God to direct your steps. Ask Him to guide you in all that you do and you will be blessed and will not falter.

Sadly, despite all this there are still many to whom God has spoken differently and yet they still reject His leading. They have allowed disbelief to cloud their eyes and hearts. God is not limited in channels of communication. Do not dismiss that dream easily or ignore that tagging on your heart. Do not lose your guidebook through negligence. Instead diligently heed all that God speaks to you.

~ CHAPTER 3 ~

THE POWER OF FAITH

JUST AS MONEY is an important currency for exchange, allowing us to buy and sell goods globally, so is faith in God's Kingdom. Faith is what allows us to receive from heaven. It is the currency that grants believers access to all that God has stored for us in the heavenly realm for every aspect of family, work, relationship and more.

In Isaiah 55:1-2, God invites all who are thirsty or hungry to come, buy and eat at no cost. He says: *"Come, all you who are thirsty, come to the waters; and you who have no money, come, buy and eat! Come, buy wine and milk without money and without cost. Why spend money on what is not bread, and your labour on what does not satisfy? Listen, listen to me, and eat what is good, and your soul will delight in the richest of fare."* This shows that in God's Kingdom we do not have to pay money for the riches of God's glory; all we have to do is approach the Lord God, our kind and heavenly Father, in faith and partake of the heavenly riches.

Faith is the central tenet that opens the stores of heaven and shuts down the wiles of the devil. If we do not have faith in God, whatever else we bring to the table is powerless. It will not take the place of faith. Without faith all our other virtues are without value. No amount of tithes, fasting or prayer can unlock heaven's doors if there is no faith attached to them. In fact Hebrews 11:6 makes it clear that *"...without faith it is impossible to please God..."*

It is in faith that we are assured of God's unconditional love. He gave us a free will and so He does not impose anything upon us. Instead, He desires that we come to Him willingly. He wants us to cultivate and sustain faith in Him which will, in turn, allow us receive from Him what He promised in His word.

~ The Difference that Faith Makes ~

FAITH CAN BE the difference between stagnation and progress. It can be the difference between living a life of lack and living in abundance. It can sometimes even mean the difference between life and death. Lack of it can stand between an individual and his/her inheritance from God.

Faith is one of the key determining factors of whether we enter our Promised Land or whether we stay in Egypt or in the desert, longing but never finding what we need in this life. Faith is the major difference in the lives of believers and unbelievers, between God's children and the children of this world, between those who have embraced Christ as their Saviour and Lord and those who have not.

It is faith that allows us to believe and know that God exists and that He works in us and for us. Faith assures us of God's active work in our lives. This same faith frees us to experience the fullness of God's grace. It empowers us and releases us to recognize the reality of a true God willing to respond to our earnest searching and supplication. He rewards our faith even as we seek Him. The word 'seek' is not used lightly. It implies both earnestness and determination; to wait on God till He comes through for us.

~ Learning from Abraham and Sarah ~

THE ENTIRE 11th chapter of the book of Hebrews is dedicated to the subject of faith. It gives us lessons using the example of the kind of faith that Abraham and Sarah demonstrated; the faith that put them into a privileged position where they were able to fully tap God's blessings. Through this couple we learn that faith elevates us to a position of privilege. Abraham's faith is a great example of what happens when one man fully relies on God.

Abraham had been promised a son; an heir to his legacy. But his youthful days were long behind him. According to scripture, he was about 100 years old. From a natural point of view, we could say that he was well past his fathering days. His wife, Sarah, was not only very old, but also barren. Every scientist will tell you that the possibility of them producing a baby was zero. For God, though, making them have a baby was so easy. The seemingly impossible situations are His specialty.

God enjoys providing solutions to problems that have no human solutions. He does it in such a way that we are left with no doubt that only He could have done it. So if you are having a challenge that you cannot solve, this is the very reason you need to entrust it to God. Consider Abraham and Sarah; the situation they were experiencing – childlessness – had no human solution. It looked impossible to solve. It was a wall that seemed too huge to climb and too strong to break. The hope for a child at a time when everything they knew was against them didn't make any human sense. It was a feat that seemed impossible. How blessed they were, that they served a God who surpasses human limits! The reason God's promise to Abraham came to pass was Abraham's faith in the God's trustworthiness, faithfulness and ability to bring to pass what He had promised (see Hebrews 11:11).

Just like Abraham and Sarah, we all face various forms of 'impossible' trials in our lives. For some, failing health or the sickness of loved ones is their predicament. There are others who face seemingly countless financial turmoil and those who never seem to have successful relationships. God wants to intervene. He who never sleeps nor slumbers is fully aware of our predicaments. He is always watching over us.

God never gives idle promises. His spoken words are never barren. They have the power to create just like He did at creation. God promised Abraham descendants that would number in the millions; as many as the stars in the sky (Genesis 15:5). It was only a matter of time and this promise would be fulfilled. His Word is able to raise us out of defeat, failure and hopelessness. Through His Word, we are securely placed on firm ground, above all human limitation and into divine providence. Stated otherwise, the purpose of God's Word is to find men who are defeated so that it can take them beyond their human limitations to their destiny. Abraham knew this and so he believed God.

In Genesis 12, God promised to bless Abraham and that through his descendants he would be a blessing to the nations. God's plan for humanity predates the creation of the world. We can safely assume that the devil was aware of these plans and so he devised a plan to short-circuit them by possibly causing Sarah to be barren. For many people, their destiny in the Lord is being contended for by the enemy. And God allows it so that at the right time He can demonstrate His glory like He demonstrated when Abraham and Sarah got a child – Isaac and through him the whole world was blessed.

Like Abraham, we must stand in faith throughout the storms of life. He believed God and reaped the fruits of his faith. Even when he was tested by God, asking him to kill his precious God-given-son as a sacrifice, he was willing to do so. I believe that in his mind, Abraham was convinced that the almighty God, the creator of the universe, would easily give him another son. And so he was willing to trust God and surrender this miracle son.

Abraham tasted fatherhood because he had faith in Him who had made the promise. We need to know and believe that God is trustworthy. He will do all that He promised to do. Trusting God is a manifestation of our faith. We therefore rest in what Christ has accomplished both on the cross and in the past. We place our full hope also in His provision in the future (See Romans 8:12-25 & Galatians 3:10-13)

We are now beneficiaries of Abraham's faith. *"Therefore the promise comes by faith so that it may be by grace and may be guaranteed to all Abraham's offspring – not only to those who are of the law, but also those who are of the faith of Abraham. He is the father of us all"* (Romans 4:16). Because of Abraham's faith, we are now part of his great lineage and hence what we need has already been guaranteed. We only need faith to receive it. When we have faith, God's grace manifests to guarantee the fulfilment of that promise. If we have no faith in what God has said, God's grace and power can hardly show up to guarantee the fulfilment of that promise. This does not mean that God is limited to our faith; there are of course cases when

He chooses to do things to manifest His glory just by His own will.

It is thus clear that the promises that God gives us can only be fulfilled if we have faith, and that whenever we have faith, God's grace and power will always prevail. Once God has promised and we have believed, He cannot afford not to fulfil His Word. To not do so would make Him a liar, something He has never been and will never be. He stands above human fallibility. Only human beings can lie. God will always honour His word.

~ Trusting in God's Promise even before Receiving ~

IMAGINE YOU RECEIVED a phone call. The person on the other side of the line introduces himself as the president of your country. He is calling to inform you that He has just appointed you as the Minister of Finance and is looking forward to working with you. What would your reaction be? Possibly you would be shocked but at the same time have heartfelt gratitude.

Now imagine that upon hearing this news, you said nothing. What would the president's thoughts be? You have just received one of the greatest appointments of your life and not a line of thanks is uttered? He would wonder what sort of person you are.

I suspect that, after the call, you would rush to your spouse to tell him/her the good news. Appropriate new clothes would be bought and speeches written in anticipation. All this would be done in preparation for your upcoming ministerial duties. You would not have been sworn in yet, but because the president himself informed you, your appointment would be surely guaranteed. He is the ultimate appointing authority and wields the power to make this happen. However, if this news was delivered to you by your next door neighbour, I doubt you would be as enthusiastic.

The book of Hebrews defines faith as being sure of what we

hope for and certain of what we do not see. How does one exhibit confidence in something that is not yet real? Hope, by definition, is an expectation of a desired outcome. How then does one act on hope alone. This can only happen when the person in whom this hope rests is so powerful and capable that their involvement assures it. Such is our hope and trust in God. He is so able that when He speaks, even before we see it come to pass, we should act as though it already has.

Romans 10:17 tells us that faith comes from hearing. Therefore the level of your faith should be dependent on who has spoken to you. If something is spoken by the human tongue, there is a chance that it will not come to pass. When the Lord speaks; because He is almighty, you can sit back and relax. It is going to happen! The promise is only as strong as the person who speaks it. The whole world and all in it was created by and belongs to God. Is He not worthy of your faith and trust?

~ CHAPTER 4 ~

THE IMPORTANCE OF A SOLID FOUNDATION

THE STRENGTH OF any structure is determined by its foundation. If you desire to build a house that will last for generations, you must ensure that its foundation is constructed from the best materials and that the construction is done to the highest standards. As Christians, we are encouraged to build upon the Rock, Jesus, and not on sand.

In the previous chapters, we discussed a lot about faith. In this Chapter, I hope to share three ingredients that ensure a solid foundation for our lives. On this foundation we can build a strong faith; the kind that will allow us to unlock the blessings of God; the kind of faith that conquers.

Foundation 1: Meditating on God's Word

~

GOD IS INCAPABLE of lying. *"God is not a man, that he should lie, nor a son of man, that he should change his mind. Does he speak and then not act? Does he promise and not fulfil?"* (Numbers 23:19). Not only does this scripture say He is not able to tell a lie; it also expressly mentions the fact that He is not man, hence He does not share in the same fickleness of humanity. He is not afraid to promise because, unlike man, He has the power to make anything come to pass. God respects His Word so much that He has exalted it above His name. When He says anything, He is bound to fulfil it. It becomes a law to Him.

It bears repeating that Romans 10:17 tells us: *"Consequently, faith comes from hearing the message, and the message is heard through the word of Christ."* Therefore, our faith must be built on truth; on what God said. The big question should be, "Did God actually say it?" If God did not say it, He is not compelled to do it. But if He said it, then He is under obligation to do it and so you can hold Him to it.

In order to constantly build our faith we need to immerse ourselves in the Word of God daily. We need to familiarize ourselves with what He has spoken through the scriptures and thus know what His promises are regarding life. Our minds, hearts and intellect become saturated in its wisdom resulting into faith. With this faith we are able to trust God more. With this faith, based on truth and governed by His will, we can do all things.

Faith that Conquers 31

Faith must not only fill our minds but should stir our hearts in order for it to have any impact on our circumstances. The distance between the heart and mind can sometimes be long but meditation on God's Word can bridge this gap. It's through meditation that the Word begins to have meaning to us.

Let's learn something from Joshua 1:1-9: *"After the death of Moses, the servant of the Lord , the Lord said to Joshua son of Nun, Moses' aide: 'Moses my servant is dead. Now then, you and all these people, get ready to cross the Jordan River into the land I am about to give to them-to the Israelites. I will give you every place where you set your foot, as I promised Moses. Your territory will extend from the desert to Lebanon, and from the great river, the Euphrates-all the Hittite country-to the Great Sea on the west. No one will be able to stand up against you all the days of your life. As I was with Moses, so I will be with you; I will never leave you nor forsake you. Be strong and courageous, because you will lead these people to inherit the land I swore to their forefathers to give them. Be strong and very courageous. Be careful to obey all the law my servant Moses gave you; do not turn from it to the right or to the left, that you may be successful wherever you go. Do not let this Book of the Law depart from your mouth; meditate on it day and night, so that you may be careful to do everything written in it. Then you will be prosperous and successful. Have I not commanded you? Be strong and courageous. Do not be terrified; do not be discouraged, for the Lord your God will be with you wherever you go."*

In the above portion of scripture, Moses had just passed on and Joshua had been chosen to lead the Israelites. Faced with the task of leading a historically troublesome nation against established kingdoms that occupied their promised homeland, Joshua turned to God. God promised him that nothing would stand against him because God Himself would fight for him. He encouraged Joshua to "be strong and courageous". He also tasked him to read the Word of God and to meditate on it daily if he, Joshua, wanted to continue enjoying God's protection and guidance. Provided that Joshua read the Word, meditated on it and obeyed it, nothing would stand in his way.

If we follow in Joshua's footsteps, we too can enjoy the kind of faith and success that was a hallmark of his life. Keeping the Word of God in your mouth simply means speaking it constantly to yourself, a sort of verbal reminder to your spirit. To meditate is to think deeply about something. It's mental 'chewing' of a concept like a cow chews curd to break it down into much finer and easier digestible portions. Mediation allows us to go over God's Word again and again, breaking it down until we have fully 'digested' it, releasing its power into our spirit and life. These processes build the sort of faith needed to possess Kingdom blessings.

In Psalm 89:33-35 God promises: *"... I will not take my love from him, nor will I ever betray my faithfulness. I will not violate my covenant or alter what my lips have uttered. Once for all, I have sworn by my holiness- and I will not lie to David".*

God is God. His words cannot be taken lightly. He describes Himself as faithful and trustworthy. He measures His words, and once spoken, He pledges to fulfil whatever He has said. This particular assurance, God gave to David. However, He extends that same assurance to us, as part of the new covenant with all those that call Him Lord.

Another excellent portion of scripture that describes and reinforces the value God puts on His word is outlined in God's call to Jeremiah. Jeremiah's authority and power to change destinies came from the fact that the words He would speak were not his. They were God's, so whatever He said would come to pass.

"The word of the Lord came to me, saying, "Before I formed you in the womb I knew you, before you were born I set you apart; I appointed you as a prophet to the nations." "Ah, Sovereign Lord," I said, "I do not know how to speak; I am only a child." But the Lord said to me, "Do not say, 'I am only a child.' You must go to everyone I send you to and say whatever I command you. Do not be afraid of them, for I am with you and will rescue you," declares the Lord. Then the Lord reached out his hand and touched my mouth and said to me, "Now, I have put my words in your mouth. See, today I appoint you over nations and kingdoms to uproot and tear down, to destroy and overthrow, to build and to plant." The Word of the Lord came to me: "What do you see, Jeremiah?" "I see the branch of an almond tree," I replied. The Lord said to me, "You have seen correctly, for I am watching to see that my word is fulfilled" (Jeremiah 1:4-12).

The above scripture reminds us that God is watching to fulfil His Word. Yet we now know that there's a part of this creation process that we have to play. This then implies that God is watching to see and hear men and women that are standing on His Word and vesting their time and faith in saying it back to Him. Many trust the words of men, so much more than the Word of our Great and Invisible God. How we could move mountains if only we believed!!

Foundation 2: Believing God's Word & Seeing His Glory

~

1 SAMUEL 15:29 states, *"He who is the Glory of Israel does not lie or change His mind; for He is not a human being, that He should change his mind."* This phrase may appear to be similar to the one we've already looked at in the previous section, but it is different. This scripture introduces to us the element of God's glory. Israel knew that God is not a man to lie or change His mind. Whenever they believed what God said, His glory showed up. Thus, our faith attracts the glory of God.

In the discussion between Martha and Jesus in John 11:25-27, Jesus mentioned the same thing to Mary and Martha when their brother Lazarus had died. Martha had not realised that Jesus who was with them was the Resurrection and the Life, and that He had the power to raise their dead brother Lazarus from the grave. So, when Jesus told them to remove the stone that was covering the grave, Martha said, "By this time there is a bad odour for he has been there for four days." But Jesus replied, "Did I not tell you that if you believed you would see the glory of God?"

Whenever we believe in what God has said, His glory shows up. The glory here implies His great power; His mighty strength, His awesomeness and His intervening grace. We are talking about His anointing that is able to break the power of witchcraft, heal the sick, reverse curses, give jobs to the unemployed, open barren wombs, defend the poor who have court cases, end bad dreams and give us prosperity in our work, businesses and investments.

Mary, the mother of Jesus, attested to the same thing in John 2:1–10 where she asked the servants to do whatever Jesus told them and it all ended with water turning into wine. What comes out of this story is that if we want to live a life of miracles, then we must constantly do whatever Jesus tells us – whether it makes sense or not. Even if we do not understand how it is going to work, as long as God has spoken, if we believe and obey what He has said, His power manifests and miracles begin to happen.

Foundation 3: Believing that God can do Anything!

~

2 SAMUEL 7:28 DECLARES, *"O Sovereign Lord, you are God! Your words are trustworthy, and you have promised these good things to your servant."* This was David's declaration after God had spoken to him. To fully understand why David said this, let's delve into the preceding story.

David had desired to build a temple; a dwelling place for God. He had felt uneasy living in a palace while God dwelt in a tent. However, God forbade him from doing so, because David was a man of war and his hands had been stained with blood. He then promised that his son would inherit the crown as kind. And he also promised that he would establish the throne of his Kingdom forever (see 2 Samuel 7:12-13).

To David, the first part of this promise made sense. Making his son king would not be difficult. However, to establish a Kingdom that would never end? That must have seemed preposterous, especially when dealing with mortal men. But David remembered that God is sovereign! He lives far above man's understanding and comprehension. He is able to do all that He wills and nothing can stop Him. His control is absolute and His power bottomless. He can bring into existence anything He so desires when He desires it.

Some situations may appear to need such grand gestures as the creation of totally new and never-before seen remedies. Can God do this? This question answers itself. God is God. There is no one greater, no one can compare! Scripture attests to creation happening today. All we need to do is actively exercise our faith.

"You have heard these things; look at them all. Will you not admit them? From now on, I will tell you of new things, of hidden things unknown to you. They are created now, and not long ago; you have not heard of them before today. So you cannot say, 'Yes, I knew of them'." (Isaiah 48:6-7). From this scripture, we see that God can create new things for us in the 'now' time. The name 'God' means that he is 'Creator'. He did not only create in the beginning; even today, He continues to create and change our situations according to our faith.

~ Build on the Above Foundations ~

THERE ARE MANY other ingredients to building a sure foundation for our faith but I single out these three because I have seen how powerfully they have transformed my life and ministry. When we build on these sure foundations, we experience God's provision and tap into unlimited power; the same power that raised Jesus from the grave. *"And his incomparably great power for us who believe. That power is like the working of his mighty strength, which he exerted in Christ when he raised him from the dead and seated him at his right hand in the heavenly realms..."* (Ephesians 1:19-20). Once that power is unleashed, the extraordinary workings and glory of God become part of our daily walk.

In Matthew 14:22-32, we are presented with an interesting story, showing Peter, a human being, walking on water. It was this same power we are talking about that made this possible. Peter saw Jesus walking on water and knew that if Jesus spoke His Word and beckoned him, he (Peter) too would receive the ability to also do the impossible i.e. walk on water. He believed that Jesus' words had the power to bring about miracles. Seeing Jesus walk on water stirred up a hunger in Peter. He desired to be just like Jesus. And so he asked Jesus to speak to him and allow him access the same power that allowed Jesus defy the waves. And so he cried out, "If it is you Lord, tell me to come."

So Jesus called back to Peter and said, "Come." God is more than pleased to respond to the requests of His beloved children. When Peter heard this command, he knew it was done. Based solely on that Word, Peter stepped out of the boat and walked on water. Obedience connected him to power which overcame all the natural laws that dictated that he would sink. His faith in Jesus' Word transformed what would be considered impossible and he was able to walk on water, as if on solid ground. That is what you enjoy when you listen to God's Word, believe it and act on it.

While God is more than happy to answer your call, an enemy waits to hear as well for the sole purpose of frustrating all that God desires. Satan was not pleased with Peter at all and caused him to shift his gaze from Jesus to the violent storm that surrounded him. He was suddenly overcome with fear and doubt. Because he was no longer focused on the Word that Jesus had spoken to him, he began to sink. He had lost connection to the power that had been sustaining him all this time.

We need to constantly defend ourselves against fear and doubt. James 1:6-8 says that anyone who lets doubt thrive is like a wave of the sea that is blown and tossed all over by the wind. Such a man is a double minded man and cannot receive from the Lord. We must renew our faith and trust on a daily basis.

This dual nature is the reason why so many do not experience their miracles. Fear, doubt and discouragement are like "demons", constantly harassing and stealing from them. When they show up, faith falters and the saint's connection to divine provision and supernatural power is lost. We must completely defeat these "demons" with the Power of Jesus and walk in faith every day.

~ CHAPTER 5 ~

ENTERING HIS REST

IN THIS WORLD we face so many challenges, trials and temptations that the only place we can find Rest is in the arms of our loving God just like he promises: *"Come to Me, all you who labour and are heavy laden, and I will give you rest" (Matthew 11:28).* Hence, it is only in the presence of God that all our burdens are off-loaded from our shoulders.

The book of Hebrews 4:1-3 says: *"Therefore, since the promise of entering His Rest still stands, let us be careful that none of you be found to have fallen short of it. For we also have had the gospel proclaimed to us, just as they did; but the message they heard was of no value to them, because those who heard did not combine it with faith. Now we who have believed enter that Rest, just as God has said, 'So I declared on oath in my anger, 'They shall never enter my Rest.' And yet His works have been finished since the creation of the world."*

To understand this scripture very well we need to recall that Sabbath means resting in the presence of God and receiving from Him whatever He promised us. Thus, God had assured the Israelites that He would give Canaan to them. He would go ahead of them so that they would defeat their enemies who were occupying the land. However, when they heard God's promises, they did not combine them with faith. They did not trust that God would fulfil His promises to them. Instead they looked at their strength, numbers and capacity in comparison with the strength of their enemies.

When faced with a challenge, if we look at the physical side of it alone, normally our minds give us reasons to be discouraged and expect the worst. In the case of the Israelites, because these people focused on themselves and looked at the power of their enemies, fear overwhelmed them, they doubted and got discouraged and so they could not enter the land of His promise. They failed to find the Rest that God had intended for them.

You can read for yourself the reported story in Deuteronomy 1:6-8 and 19-35. From this story, we learn that God punished the children of Israel because they did not trust in Him and that they had doubted His power even when He demonstrated it to them through signs and wonders while they passed through the desert. He thus said they would never enter Canaan. He took back all of them to the desert and they kept on moving in circles until they all died in the desert except Joshua and Caleb who had believed in God and given a good report of faith about the Promised Land.

~ The Testimony of Caleb ~

WE LEARN A lot from reflecting on the story of Caleb as reported in Joshua 14:6-15. From this story we realise that the reason Caleb was set apart so that he may enter his Rest, the Promised Land was because when he was sent in to spy the land, he brought a report according to his convictions. The rest (except Joshua) died and failed to enter the Promised Land.

Caleb's conviction was that yes, the land had occupants who seemed strong and mighty, but that the God he had known was faithful to His promise and was able to defeat their enemies and give the land to the Israelites. It is important for us as believers to constantly live under this conviction no matter what situations confront us. The mistake the others made was to look at the circumstances in the land and so they brought back a report that made the people's hearts melt with fear. Because of this fear, God did not allow them to enter their Rest.

Caleb teaches us to follow the Lord wholeheartedly. God challenges us to either follow Him wholeheartedly or not follow Him at all. There's no being lukewarm; neither hot nor cold. Because Caleb had followed God wholeheartedly, God gave him a promise that He would give him long life so that he would come and inherit the land. In this testimony of Caleb, we see that God was indeed faithful to Caleb and He kept him alive for 45 more years while the rest of the people died. Again this is fulfilment of scripture, just as God promised that when we serve Him and live by His Word, He gives us long life.

Caleb also testifies that at 85 years of age, he was still as strong as he was when he was 40 years old. At that age, he still felt strong enough to fight and defeat his enemies. Here, we see another important benefit of living by faith: God does not only give us long life; He also blesses us so that in our old age we still live a qualitative life and enjoy good health. Thus, even in old age, God keeps us strong and productive. We see this promise fulfilled in the lives of several other Biblical figures such as Abraham who received his promised son, Isaac, at the age of 100 years; and Moses who was called at the age of 40 and led the people of Israel when he was already in his 80s.

We continue to learn from Caleb to always claim what God has promised us. In fact, the land that God had promised him was that belonging to the Anakites (the giants in the land) that other Israelites were so scared of. The specific place that God gave Caleb belonged to a man called Aba who was the strongest man among the Anakites. It must have been one of the best places in the whole land and one of the most guarded. But Caleb was not afraid to claim that land. He believed that with the Lord on his side he would drive them out and conquer the land just like God had promised him. When you have faith, it does not matter what you are fighting against; what matters is who is fighting for you i.e. God.

Quite often we believe God for the fulfilment of certain promises but when the promises take long to get fulfilled we change our minds and console ourselves that it must be God's will for us not to get that which we desire. Well, it may be God's will, but sometimes it's not His will at all, but rather our weak ability to persevere and patiently wait on Him. For Caleb to have insisted on claiming the land that God had promised him 45 years earlier is a great lesson to us. Caleb was convinced beyond any reasonable doubt that once God has made a promise, He cannot change His mind when it comes to fulfilling it no matter how long it takes.

Faith that Conquers

Caleb's experience also teaches us that when we live by faith and obedience to God, the inheritance we get becomes ours, our children's and the children of our children. Thus, when we are working hard, enduring challenges and keeping in the walk of faith, we are not doing it for ourselves alone but also for our descendants.

Just like Caleb entered his Rest, the same promise for the church to enter that kind of Rest is still available to every believer today. We just need to be very careful that none of us is found to have fallen short of the requirements. The church has the gospel preached and we have God's promises just like Israel had God's promise when they were entering the Promised Land of Canaan. If we stick to those promises, we shall surely inherit that Promised Land.

~ CHAPTER 6 ~

ALL POSSIBLE WITH GOD

THROUGHOUT THE PREVIOUS chapters, we have consistently seen that God proves His ability to work out events as He so wishes. There is nothing that is outside of is control and no situation that takes Him by surprise. All bow before His command. The universe sits in His hand.

The knowledge of God should strengthen our faith. We are different from those that serve idols and other gods that are made by the hands of man and that neither speak nor hear.

Scripture is replete with testimonies of God's people. The barren bore children, water turned into wine, the dead lived again and those cast into flames were untouched. That's the kind of God we believe in.

~ God has already done It! ~

WHAT PEACE IS ours when we know that all that God promises are already done! It's a completed work of Jesus Christ. He paid the price so that as you pray, you can have complete assurance that it is finished. In the spiritual realm it is already a reality. We simply need to see it in faith and with clarity and then know what we ought to do.

"His divine power has given us everything we need for life and godliness through our knowledge of him who called us by his own glory and goodness. Through these he has given us his very great and precious promises, so that through them you may participate in the divine nature and escape the corruption in the world caused by evil desires" (2Peter 1:3-4). In this scripture, Peter is telling us that God has granted us all that we need for life and godliness. Everything we will ever need is taken care of. These needs are normally two fold; those that are physical for life on earth and those we need for a godly life. Fulfilment in these areas leads to a lifestyle that pleases God.

When God provides in both aspects of our need, we become materially successful as well as spiritually strong to accomplish God's will. It strengthens our relationship with our Father because we grow in faith and are able to overcome those things that seek to destroy us. Victory becomes the hallmark of our physical reality.

In other words we receive sustenance both for our physical needs as well as for our spiritual needs through our knowledge of Christ. He is the embodiment of the Word that is our key to unfathomable power. Once we are one with that power, everything is within reach to us.

Faith that Conquers

~ Dead to the World but Alive in Christ ~

WHEN WE OBEY God through faith, we are connected to power that allows us to participate in the divine nature of God. Following God's blueprint allows us to escape the frustrating cycle of worldly methodology. When we become Born Again, we are filled by the Holy Spirit and receive God's nature that allows us do things in a way that reflects God's nature. How I love 'Touching Heaven, Changing Earth', a song done by Hillsong! It makes me feel this divine-human encounter that we are talking about.

God's nature resurrects even what is dead. He brings life where there is none. Calling things that are not as if they are is faith in action. As Christians we should not focus on our circumstance but instead choose to set our eyes on our magnificent God, in whom we can do all things! If we see with the eyes of the Spirit, we will not be doubtful. This sets us up to live victoriously. Like another song proclaims, we can declare: "Let the weak say I am strong; let the poor say I am rich..." because God's power transforms our weaknesses into strength, our curses into blessings, our darkness into day and our poverty into riches.

In Ezekiel Chapter 37:1-10 we find one of the most recognizable and bizarre scenes the Bible ever describes. Let me present it as it is – lengthy but powerful:

"The hand of the LORD was upon me, and he brought me out by the Spirit of the LORD and set me in the middle of a valley; it was full of bones. He led me back and forth among them, and I saw a great many bones on the floor of the valley, bones that were very dry. He asked me, "Son of man, can these bones live?" I said, "O Sovereign LORD, you alone know." Then he said to me, "Prophesy to these bones and say to them, 'Dry bones, hear the word of the LORD! This is what

the Sovereign LORD says to these bones: I will make breath enter you, and you will come to life. I will attach tendons to you and make flesh come upon you and cover you with skin; I will put breath in you, and you will come to life. Then you will know that I am the LORD.' "So I prophesied as I was commanded. And as I was prophesying, there was a noise, a rattling sound, and the bones came together, bone to bone. I looked, and tendons and flesh appeared on them and skin covered them, but there was no breath in them. Then he said to me, "Prophesy to the breath; prophesy, son of man, and say to it, 'This is what the Sovereign LORD says: Come from the four winds, O breath, and breathe into these slain, that they may live.' So I prophesied as he commanded me, and breath entered them; they came to life and stood up on their feet – a vast army."

Here we see a valley full of bones that were dry and devoid of life. They are the perfect description of "death". In the midst of this, God commands the prophet Ezekiel to speak to these bones. Right before his eyes, the bones reconnect, gather flesh and sinews and before he knows it, human beings are standing in the valley as alive as Ezekiel himself. When we hear God's words and speak them out, they have the power to change situations. In my experience as a minister, I have learned that many times God's workings in our lives may come in stages and one must speak into the situation over and over again, until the miracle is complete.

~ The Testimony of Healing ~

I ONCE HAD a chance to exercise all that I had been preaching. After a session in which I had spoken, I was approached by a sister in the Lord. She had questions about speaking prophetically into our lives. Did it really work? Whilst talking, she shared that her cousin was sick. We took this as a chance to try out our faith. We drove to her aunt's home.

Upon our arrival, we discovered that another child in the home had fallen ill and had been taken to hospital. The parents of the child, Aunt and Uncle, were therefore not home. However her cousin was there.

The sick girl was wheeled into the room in a wheelchair. Her limp hands hung from her sides while her feet dragged along the floor. She could not control her own oral muscles and so sat drooling from her mouth. She was unable to speak. Her malady was so bad she was forced to drop out of school. To the team and I, this looked like another valley of dry bones, another impossible situation. We encouraged each other in the Lord. We knew it was God who worked miracles, not us. I suggested we pray for each part of her body, prophetically speaking into them and commanding that they regain their full functionality.

Armed with faith we began to speak God's Word to her. We spoke to her mouth and to her cheek muscles that they would speak again and declare the goodness of God. We spoke to her neck and declared strength that it fulfil its purpose. We spoke to her arms, her shoulders and back and declared strength back into her muscles. We spoke into her arms and commanded their muscles to regain strength, declaring that they would work and that God would constantly bless the work of those hands and that they would touch God's people, bringing healing to them. We broke every yoke of the enemy over her life and declared that by the cross of Jesus all her enemies were defeated and Jesus paid the price for her to be totally delivered. We declared that every aspect of her life that was affected would be restored and that she would live to declare the message of the gospel.

After we had prayed for about an hour, there was nothing that showed our prayers had worked. The family thanked us and we left, albeit a little discouraged. Two weeks later, I received a call from the little girl's mother. She was excited and in tears. "Pastor Nicholas!" she exclaimed, "You can't believe it! She is walking and running. She has even gone back to school!" It was like the Lord stayed behind as we left, working our confession of faith into being till she was completely restored.

We have the power to speak life into any situation. The church is filled with many such situations that look like the "valley of dry bones" These may be poverty, failing health, bad relationships or other oppressive situations. But God demonstrates to us believers that we have the power to turn around any situation by speaking His Word. Even you can prophetically speak to your situation and see the fulfilment of God's promises in your life.

While praying we need to remember that God responds at will as He sees fit. When God says it will be, it will! Our faith and our actions could change the course of God's will. God is God, but He is not a tyrant. He gives us room to re-create our situation with Him. It is therefore important that we make all decisions concerning our lives and our faith carefully, reverently and deliberately. Our choices, our decisions and our faith could deter us from His good and perfect will or turn Him to favour us and intervene in a sad situation.

"In those days Hezekiah became ill and was at the point of death. The prophet Isaiah son of Amoz went to him and said, "This is what the Lord says: Put your house in order, because you are going to die; you will not recover." Hezekiah turned his face to the wall and prayed to the Lord, "Remember, O Lord, how I have walked before you faithfully and with wholehearted devotion and have done what is good in your eyes." And Hezekiah wept bitterly. Then the word of the Lord came to Isaiah: "Go and tell Hezekiah, 'This is what the Lord, the God of your father David, says: I have heard your prayer and seen your tears; I will add fifteen

years to your life" (2 Kings 20:1-5).

By his faithfulness to and love for God, King Hezekiah earned the Lord's favour and altered the duration of his life. This too, is a possibility with God. He is God, and will do as He chooses. We are certain of this; that when we pray and believe in accordance to His will, He will answer! Sometimes His answers are immediate or take a while. Remembering my experience with the sick girl, we may not have seen immediate physical signs that our prayer had been answered. In fact we were a little discouraged. Nonetheless we held to our belief that God does answer when His children pray. Many of us lose out because we do not hold out in faith until we see the result.

~ CHAPTER 7 ~

PROMISES ARE LIKE SEEDS

MANY TIMES IN scripture, God likens His work to seed. This is no accident. Seeds are a symbol of life, growth and patience. In the proceeding chapter we will try to focus on how to patiently tend good seed and how to ensure that it grows and fully blooms.

Every farmer knows that his bounty will not come instantly. Patience is his greatest ally. We must understand as believers that in life we will not have all we want when we want it. Like a farmer we shall have to wait patiently. This is how God designed it.

~ Dying First Like Seeds ~

As mentioned previously, GOD'S PROMISES ARE often likened to seeds in scripture. When you embrace a promise it's planted in your heart like a seed. This promise undergoes the same process that a planted seed does. Before a seed sprouts into life, it must first die. Within the soil this seed rots. Strangely enough this dying is what gives way to life. In such a way even when we see "death", faith allows our seed to defy it and bring forth life.

It should therefore not be surprising when sometimes the situations we pray for seem to get worse before they get better. If you recall in earlier chapters, I shared how my finances seemed to worsen after I had become Born Again. I had the option of giving up and surrendering to my situation or holding on until the promise manifested. I chose the latter and I was rewarded. We often times respond in fear and discouragement when faced with a seeming stall on God's part. But with steadfastness and perseverance, He always comes through.

Faith is not the only thing that goes through a similar process of a germinating seed. Businesses and many other ventures in life also go through such situations. Many go through seasons of no profits at all and at this time many abandon their visions oblivious that if they had waited a little longer, their visions would have come to life and propel them to success.

~ Living by Faith, not by Sight ~

WE SHOULD STAND fast even when we are unable to see physical results, because we are called to live by faith and not by sight.[3] God gives us spiritual eyes that we may see past the natural realm. That's what faith is all about; believing even before we have seen physically. We know that when a farmer plants, the seedling does not sprout and bud immediately. However, he does not spend his days fretting, that the seed has been planted and yet there is nothing above the ground to show for it. Instead, he sets about

---
3 Hebrews 10:38: "But my righteous one will live by faith. And if he shrinks back, I will not be pleased with him."

doing whatever else he has to, believing that at the appointed time, the seeds will sprout.

Not all seed germinates at the same time. In the Bible we find different versions of the phrase, "in the fullness of time". This is important because God answers us in varied ways. Sometimes the more valuable the seed, the longer the seed will take to mature and bear fruit. Coffee takes five years to bear fruit. The amount of time it takes before you see results is no indicator of whether it shall or shall not come to pass.

God's promises are seeds that are planted in our souls. We should allow them proper time to germinate, grow and produce fruit. We have to hold onto God's Word while we ride through the situations that might discourage us. Please persevere and keep walking in faith. Your turn will come to harvest.

We may not always understand the process that promises go through to manifest. All we need is faith till we see them manifest. This is very different from a lot of current church teaching which emphasizes instant miracles. I do not deny that such miracles do exist and happen especially in situations where God's glory needs to be demonstrated but often times it will take some time before we see our "seeds" of faith come to fruition.

~ When Faith seems Unproductive ~

WHAT IS OUR response when we have faith for a particular outcome but nothing happens? Let's consider Jesus Christ in anticipation of His gruesome death. *"They went to a place called Gethsemane, and Jesus said to his disciples, "Sit here while I pray." He took Peter, James and John along with him, and he began to be deeply distressed and troubled. "My soul is overwhelmed with sorrow to the point of death," he said to them. "Stay here and keep watch." Going a little farther, he fell to the ground and prayed that if possible the hour might pass from him. 'Abba, Father," he said, "everything is possible for you. Take this cup from me. Yet not what I will, but what you will' "* (Mark 14:32-36).

This passage describes the emotions Jesus Christ went through before the crucifixion. He knew what was to come, and being God, He knew it was the ultimate price for our freedom. This knowledge did not make the future any easier to expect or to endure. Our Lord, agonized over what He knew was to happen. If the bad experience could be avoided, He asked that God the Father shield Him from it. However, it was God's will that Jesus go through what He did; for the greater good. We are enjoying the result of that greater good today, as Gentile sons and daughters. But this good came through God's painful sacrifice. Mary, Jesus' mother, and all His friends endured unbearable loss, albeit for three days. But today, we are free!! We are His! Sometimes our great omniscient God knows the good that can come from terrible things happening. He lets them happen for our good and for His glory. We must trust His immeasurable and insatiable love for us. If He lets it happen, it is for a purpose. It might be best known to Him then, but it is there and He is great and He is good. Let us not give up, but rather, pray for endurance through those difficult times.

So, if there are situations that come into our lives and do not change even when we have prayed and exercised our faith, we must trust that God knows why the story is going that way. Ultimately, *"we know that in all things God works for the good of those who love him, who have been called according to his purpose"* (Romans 8:28).

Another example is Paul's experience when God gave him a thorn in his flesh. *"To keep me from becoming conceited because of these surpassingly great revelations, there was given me a thorn in my flesh, a messenger of Satan, to torment me. Three times I pleaded with the Lord to take it away from me. But he said to me, 'My grace is sufficient for you, for my power is made perfect in weakness.' Therefore I will boast all the more gladly about my weaknesses, so that Christ's power may rest on me. That is why, for Christ's sake, I delight in weaknesses, in insults, in hardships, in persecutions, in difficulties. For when I am weak, then I am strong"* (2 Corinthians 12:7-10). We realize that God gave him this thorn to keep him from becoming conceited so that he may be humbled to the place of total dependence on God. He says he prayed three times and pleaded with the Lord to take it away, but God said that He would instead give him the grace to bear it because God's power is made perfect in weakness.

It is laughable that many think God is defeated when their answers delay. He is all-seeing and all-knowing not to mention all powerful. In scripture He declares: *"Is there anything too hard for me?"* There is a reason for the delay, continue to trust and rest in God. Don't let a temporary delay or an unexpected outcome rob you of joy and peace. James encourages us: *"Consider it pure joy, (my brothers), whenever you face trials of many kinds, because you know that the testing of your faith develops perseverance"* (James 1:2-3).

Scripture admonishes us to be happy when we face many trials. God uses them to shape character and help us develop perseverance or overcome most of our sinful nature. While we may not know how or when our miracles happen, we are assured that something is already changing inside of us.

God sometimes uses pain and suffering as tools to teach us His ways. We readily turn to God when humbled by suffering. *"Although the Lord gives you the bread of adversity and the water of affliction, your teachers will be hidden no more; with your own eyes you will see them. Whether you turn to the right or to the left, your ears will hear a voice behind you, saying, "This is the way; walk in it"* (Isaiah 30:20-21). Suffering makes us more attentive to God's voice.

Thus many situations we go through weaken the flesh and make us more willing to live carefully and to turn to God daily for help. When we do, God strengthens us with power so that we can be more effective in our calling. We should never let such distractions divert us from our life's purpose.

~ Challenges shouldn't kill the Seed ~

TWO BIBLE PERSONALITIES come to mind when I think of men who kept the seed alive despite incredible odds; Paul and Stephen. Paul was being led to Rome where he was to preach salvation to the Romans. Despite many people trying to dissuade him, he insisted on going on. God had sent him. He was bearing precious seed and had to go plant it in Rome.

In Acts 27, the ship that was transporting Paul sailed into a storm. According to scripture, they faced several challenges and were driven forward before a merciless storm. Many of the crew despaired but Paul encouraged them. They would not die even though they would lose the ship. An angel had visited Him in the night and assured him of this. Even after being beached after the shipwreck, Paul, while adding wood to a fire, is bitten by a venomous snake but it did not kill him. He had a mission to accomplish in Rome and nothing would deter him – not even death itself. God had promised it and God would see it through.

The story of Stephen is very well narrated in the book of Acts chapter 7, verses 54 to 59. He was the first recorded Christian martyr. It's recorded that when the mob attacked him, he looked up and saw heaven open and Jesus standing at the right hand of God the father. With that vision burned into his heart he faced death without fear. He had seen heaven and with that knowledge he stepped into a new realm. That revelation allowed him to surpass human notions and even forgive and pray for his tormentors, even as they hurled rocks at him. This is a similar scene at Golgotha, Calvary. Jesus, like Stephen, looked to the heaven and prayed for his crucifiers. He focused on the victory ahead and not on his circumstances.

This vision sustained Stephen through the unimaginable pain of being stoned. I can only imagine his pain and suffering. For him to raise himself to his knees and focus long enough to make any prayer let alone one of forgiveness and mercy for his enemies is testimony to the power that vision had granted him. If Stephen could live through that kind of suffering, what about the little skirmishes we have? Faced with sudden demise or accident, our exclamations are unbelievable. Stephen bore precious seed in his soul and knew that his blood would be the "water" that would allow this seed to grow and him to enter his rest.

~ CHAPTER 8 ~

ARE WE READY TO POSSESS THE LAND?

I HOPE THAT by now we are aware that God created each of us with a purpose in mind. I hope we also know that not only did He give us purpose, but He also provided a way for us to achieve it as well. I believe the dreams God gives us are part of this plan. Through your dreams you are able to identify which promises in God's Word apply to you and through confessing them are able to inherit your "promised land".

The story of Joseph illustrates how dreams are pivotal in guiding our destiny, and how, when we diligently follow God's leading, we step into our destiny. Joseph's dreams were a revelation of God's purpose for His life, which was to save His people from starvation. Joseph believed the dreams but so did Satan. Through the actions of his brothers, Satan sought to thwart God's plans. When that did not work, he used sexual temptation and the anger of a scorned woman to try and get between Joseph and his destiny.

With the memories of these dreams vivid in his heart and mind, Joseph determined to stay righteous, knowing that this was the only way for him to walk in God's will for his life. Joseph knew that if he persevered in living a Holy Life, God would always work things out for his good. Throughout his trials, Joseph trusted God to come to his aid and to fulfil the dreams that He had given him. They could delay, but they would surely come to pass.

We already know how Joseph's story ends. He rose to be one of the most powerful men in Egypt, saved his family from annihilation and set the foundation for the rest of the salvation story. When God fulfils His plan for you even enemies bow before you.

~ Contending with the Enemy ~

AS WE CONTEND with the enemy, God is not asleep. Just because God promised it, does not mean you shall not have to fight to keep it. Many times we face trials along our promise journey, but all that the devil intends for evil, God works for our good as promised in Romans 8:28. Joseph was sold into slavery, and was later falsely accused and thrown in jail. All the while, these events acted as catalysts that propelled Joseph ever closer to God's purpose for his life.

There are many situations we are bound to face as the enemy seeks to discourage us and make us doubt God's love and Will for our lives. He will bring discouragement, failure and misfortune to try to discredit God's Word over your life. But praise God, Hallelujah! We are assured that nothing can separate us from God's love – not even death. *"Who shall separate us from the love of Christ? Shall trouble or hardship or persecution or famine or nakedness*

Faith that Conquers

or danger or sword?" (Romans 8:35).

Like Shadrach, Meshach and Abednego, we will have to constantly declare, *"O Nebuchadnezzar, we do not need to defend ourselves before you in this matter. If we are thrown into the blazing furnace, the God we serve is able to save us from it, and he will rescue us from your hand, O king. But even if he does not, we want you to know, O king, that we will not serve your gods or worship the image of gold you have set up"* (Daniel 3:16-18).

As we strive towards our promised land, we must persevere. We must believe God no matter what. We must hold onto the promise even as we believe that God will keep His Word to us. God consistently admonishes us to persevere because it builds faith in us. He knows the path towards our goal is littered with all manner of traps and snares. We are constantly assailed by the servants of Satan along our way to try and get us to give up and give in to despair and disbelief. If you do not persevere you are liable to abandon your dream before it has a chance to come to life.

The promises contained in God's Word are part of the arsenal we can use when we find ourselves in a spiritual pinch. A good example is in the book of Ephesians 6:10-13: *"Finally, be strong in the Lord and in his mighty power. Put on the full armour of God so that you can take your stand against the devil's schemes. For our struggle is not against flesh and blood, but against the rulers, against the authorities, against the powers of this dark world and against the spiritual forces of evil in the heavenly realms. Therefore put on the full armour of God, so that when the day of evil comes, you may be able to stand your ground, and after you have done everything, to stand."*

It is vital that we remain prepared so that when that day comes we should be fully clothed in the divine raiment of God's Word. With the sword of the Spirit, we can go on the offensive and fight off the enemy. Regardless of how powerful our present adversary is, none is mightier than God and His Word!

Like an army preparing for battle, we must amass God's promises in our hearts and spirits. Like savings in the bank, we can call on these reserves in a case of emergency. Reading and meditating on God's Word is like building up reserves in our spirit for that day when we need help. The Holy Spirit, using these reserves, is able to call up scripture to memory that we can speak out and counter any and all attacks of the enemy. We should not wait for the heat of battle to start searching for God's Word but instead be prepared always.

There is no growth in the Spirit without some sort of struggle. We cannot inherit the Promised Land without confronting some giants in our life. Sometimes these giants are our own perceptions and fears. Sometimes we see the devil hindering us and sometimes we are our own hindrance. We need wisdom and discernment so we know what portion of scripture to apply to what challenge lest we use the wrong promise and see no results.

~ Learning from Hannah's Experience ~

IN THE BOOK of 1 Samuel, we are introduced to Hannah, wife of Elkanah, a priest in the temple. She was unable to bear children and this haunted her. She endured scorn and abuse from her co-wife Peninnah who had children.

Tired and fed up with the scorn and ridicule she went to the One person who could raise her out of her predicament. She knew that before God she was special and valued. In her desperation she cried out for a child and promised that if indeed she had a son she would dedicate him to Yahweh's service.

Our dreams sometimes are revelations from God. You might dream of doing mighty things and many will dismiss this as a mere dream, yet God is actually speaking to us. These dreams, unlike usual dreams, leave us unsettled and uncomfortable to the point that we have no choice but to follow them through.

Consumed by her desire for a child Hannah poured her heart out to God in earnest prayer. So passionate was her prayer that many thought she was intoxicated. Before God we need not be ashamed. We are standing before our Father and thus we must freely express ourselves. Putting our all before the feet of Jesus is a demonstration of our faith; it's us saying, "Here, no one else can do this. I bring it to you."

~ With faith we see more than others can see ~

IN 2 KINGS 6: 8-17, we see a similar demonstration of faith, like that of Hannah, by Prophet Elisha. And here goes the story:

"Now the king of Aram was at war with Israel. After conferring with his officers, he said, "I will set up my camp in such and such a place." The man of God sent word to the king of Israel: "Beware of passing that place, because the Arameans are going down there." So the king of Israel checked on the place indicated by the man of God. Time and again Elisha warned the king, so that he was on his guard in such places. This enraged the king of Aram. He summoned his officers and demanded of them, "Will you not tell me which of us is on the side of the king of Israel?" "None of us, my lord the king," said one of his officers, "but Elisha, the prophet who is in Israel, tells the king of Israel the very words you speak in your bedroom." "Go, find out where he is," the king ordered, "so I can send men and capture him." The report came back: "He is in Dothan." Then he sent horses and chariots and a strong force there. They went by night and surrounded the city. When the servant of the man of God got up and went out early the next morning, an army with horses and chariots had surrounded the city.

"Oh, my lord, what shall we do?" the servant asked. "Don't be afraid," the prophet answered. "Those who are with us are more than those who are with them." And Elisha prayed, "O Lord, open his eyes so he may see." Then the Lord opened the servant's eyes, and he looked and saw the hills full of horses and chariots of fire all around Elisha."

The major reason Elisha was able to operate at a much higher level than most of the other Israelites was his faith. He was able to see and hear things than many were oblivious to. Through his faith he had access to a plane that many are just simply unaware of. This ability made him indispensible to the armies of Israel. His constant guidance allowed them to be victorious in battle after battle. Their enemies were so thoroughly annoyed that they figured that to have any hope of winning they would have to get rid of Elisha. Imagine a whole nation mobilized an army to go after one man, but even that plan was doomed to failure.

When the residents of Aram woke up that morning, I am sure the last thing they expected to see was an army encamped around their town. Elisha's servant, on hearing that his master was the focus of the mass mobilization, was terrified; but Elisha calmly told his servant to be at peace. Surrounded and outnumbered by men, he was unfazed, for he could see that his heavenly allies so far outnumbered those that had sought his life.

Faced with his servant's fear, Elisha dealt with it head on. Fear is one of the biggest and many times the most effective tool the enemy uses against the faithful. Elisha encouraged his servant with these words: "Those who are with us are greater than those that are against us." He then prayed that His servant's eyes would be opened and, lo and behold the hills around them were filled with heavenly hosts ready to do battle on behalf of Elisha and his righteous cause.

Regardless of the numbers surrounding you, look up and

Faith that Conquers

know that there is One who is determined to see you win and will always come to your aid. He is always right on time! God is able to change any situation. We must learn to tap into the resources that He has made available to us for Life and Godliness.

Luckily for us God did not build the foundations of His Kingdom on human knowledge or skill. So our individual attributes are unimportant in the face of His plans. All He seeks is a willing and obedient heart. Furthermore He is more than pleased to give you the fruits of His promise. *"Do not be afraid, little flock, for your Father has been pleased to give you the kingdom"* (Luke 12:32).

You are a child of the Kingdom. You are under the sovereign protection of God. It's all about Him now. Trust Him; connect with His Word regarding your predicament. What He declares is eternal and all that stands in your way is temporal. It can and will be turned around to make God's purposes come to pass.

In today's world, we often trust in money, power, fame, science and success. We tend to believe that these can bring us the happiness, peace, security and the future we desire. But God wants us to learn to trust in His promises and providence for He is able to provide all our needs today and even give us the kind of future we envision. That's what faith is about.

~ Seek God's wisdom ~

BECAUSE WE ARE in a world that is not our own, we need the help of the One person who knows this world inside and out. And that's God. We need to depend on His wisdom as we navigate this tricky path. Like soldiers behind enemy lines we need the support of our headquarters. From them we get spiritual surveillance and guidance. Keeping these channels of communication open to receive divine wisdom should be a daily task.

Here is God's promise to you and I in Isaiah 48:17-18: *"This is what the Lord says – your Redeemer, the Holy One of Israel: 'I am the Lord your God, who teaches you what is best for you, who directs you in the way you should go. If only you had paid attention to my commands, your peace would have been like a river, your righteousness like the waves of the sea."*

God further promises in Isaiah 42:16: *"I will lead the blind by ways they have not known, along unfamiliar paths I will guide them; I will turn the darkness into light before them and make the rough places smooth. These are the things I will do; I will not forsake them."*

God's wisdom and guidance is perfectly demonstrated in the life of King Solomon. In Proverbs 4, we see how God used his father to teach him the value of wisdom when he was still a young boy. Proverbs 4:1-7 says: *"Listen, my sons, to a father's instruction; pay attention and gain understanding. I give you sound learning, so do not forsake my teaching. When I was a boy in my father's house, still tender, and an only child of my mother, he taught me and said, 'Lay hold of my words with all your heart; keep my commands and you will live. Get wisdom, get understanding; do not forget my words or swerve from them. Do not forsake wisdom, and she will protect you; love her, and she will watch over you. Wisdom is supreme; therefore get wisdom. Though it cost all you have, get understanding.'"*

Clearly, his walk with wisdom started at an early age. Through his father, Solomon learned the supreme importance of wisdom above all things. So great was his respect for wisdom that when asked what he desired the most by God he asked for wisdom.

"At Gibeon the Lord appeared to Solomon during the night in a dream, and God said, "Ask for whatever you want me to give you." Solomon answered, "You have shown great kindness to your servant, my father David, because he was faithful to you and righteous and upright in heart. You have continued this great kindness to him and have given

him a son to sit on his throne this very day. "Now, O Lord my God, you have made your servant king in place of my father David. But I am only a little child and do not know how to carry out my duties. Your servant is here among the people you have chosen, a great people, too numerous to count or number. So give your servant a discerning heart to govern your people and to distinguish between right and wrong. For who is able to govern this great people of yours?" The Lord was pleased that Solomon had asked for this. So God said to him, "Since you have asked for this and not for long life or wealth for yourself, nor have asked for the death of your enemies but for discernment in administering justice, I will do what you have asked. I will give you a wise and discerning heart, so that there will never have been anyone like you, nor will there ever be. Moreover, I will give you what you have not asked for-both riches and honour-so that in your lifetime you will have no equal among kings. And if you walk in my ways and obey my statutes and commands as David your father did, I will give you a long life" (1 Kings 3:5-14).

Here he was, given the freedom to ask for anything; (we have already learned that when God says anything He means it). Instead of riches, power or even the defeat of his enemies Solomon asked for wisdom. So impressed was God by this that He bestowed upon Solomon all the other riches that he had not asked for, including long life.

When presented with an opportunity, we should discard all desire for quick worldly gains and instead seek longer lasting virtues. I pray that we will always seek that which sets us on the path to eternal life. While we may not have a physical audience with God we still have access to His Word and through it access to Him, and to unfathomable wisdom.

We must also seek to put our faith to action. Knowledge of God's promises is not enough. We cannot afford to sit and wait. Instead, we should take initiative. Sometimes this might mean making an open declaration or starting that thing God has placed on your heart with the few resources available. As we step forward, God's grace meets us along the way and our dreams and destinies slowly, but surely, are built into realities. God's wisdom should transform us into men and women of action as we seek to live according to God's Word and purpose for our lives.

"As the body without the spirit is dead, so faith without deeds is dead" (James 2:26). James said this to emphasize what he had already said that *"...faith by itself, if it is not accompanied by action, is dead"* (James 2:17).

As we come to the end of this book, I also want to make that emphasis: your faith alone, if not backed by action in the right direction, won't conquer; it is faith with the right deeds that conquers.

~ NOTES ~

~ NOTES ~

~ NOTES ~

~ NOTES ~

www.ingramcontent.com/pod-product-compliance
Lightning Source LLC
Chambersburg PA
CBHW031416040426
42444CB00005B/589